I AM ADOPTED

by Susan Lapsley

& illustrated by
Michael Charlton

THE BODLEY HEAD
LONDON

OTHER SPECIAL SITUATION PICTURE BOOKS

ANNA
(about a child with eczema)

THE HOUSE WHERE JACK LIVES
(about life in a children's home)

MIKE
(about a boy who wets his bed)

MY FAMILY
(about a one-parent family)

SUZY
(about a partially sighted child)

WHEEZY
(about a child with asthma)

ISBN 0 370 02032 4
Printed in Great Britain for
The Bodley Head Ltd
32 Bedford Square, London WC1B 3EL
by Cambus Litho, East Kilbride
First published 1974
Reprinted 1976, 1982, 1984, 1985, 1988

My name is Charles.
I am adopted.

So is my sister, Sophie.

She is only little.

I have a tractor.

It was a birthday present.

My friend is
called Mark.

He often comes to
play with me.

Do you know
what adopted means?

I do.

It means
we were given to
Mummy and Daddy

when we were little.

And they brought us home

to make a family.

Now I'm much bigger

I can play a tune on Granny's piano.

Sophie and I make lots of things together

and we feed our
rabbit, Benjy.

Mummy lets us do cooking sometimes

and I work with
Daddy on the car.

Daddy comes home at tea-time

and helps us
have our bath.

Every night we
have a bed-time
story before
we go to
sleep

Adoption means belonging.

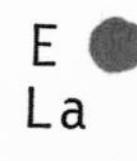